Paper Clip Jewelry

Olivia Toliver

Mud Puddle Books

NEW YORK

Paper Clip Jewelry
by Olivia Toliver

© 2007 by Mud Puddle Books, Inc.

Published by
Mud Puddle Books, Inc.
54 W. 21st Street
Suite 601
New York, NY 10010
info@mudpuddlebooks.com

ISBN: 978-1-60311-052-5

Printed in China.

table of contents

introduction

As long as there have been people, there has been jewelry! Shells, animal teeth, and carved stone were all used in primitive cultures as functional forms of adornment. Just like the people that wore it, jewelry evolved over time. Jewels and gems were added to give a girl that extra pizzazz. Today, you don't need expensive trinkets to have the most fabulous jewelry. You can create your own using a number of easy-to-find, easy-to-use materials. Swank for the hippest party, mellow for just hanging out, or trendy for the look of the moment—it's your style, so you choose!

This book will teach you how to take the most everyday item, the paper clip, and transform it into unique-as-you-are earrings, necklaces, backpack tags, and more. These fun projects are ones you'll love to make and love to wear. ***Jewelry. Want it, need it, gotta have it!***

Chapter 1
Designer Tips, Techniques, and Secrets

Tools for Making Designer Jewlery

As with any craft project, it's important to have the right tools. The right tools for the job make designing jewelry both easy and fun. Without them, it's often nothing more than a very frustrating and unsuccessful experience.

Tools for making paper clip jewelry are easy-to-find, inexpensive, and will last you forever, if they're taken care of. The following supplies are the basics, all of which can be created at home or found in your local craft and hobby store.

Work Area

A special place to make your jewelry is both fun and practical, especially if it's one where you can safely leave your beads and tools out. This way, you will not have to take those extra minutes to put things away when it comes time to stop making jewelry and help around the house, do homework, or meet up with a friend.

Your workspace should be safe for small children and animals. Beads can be a choking hazard, and young children can potentially harm themselves with some of the tools used. If you are unsure about how to use some of your tools when you first begin, ask for help! With proper direction, you will soon be an expert.

The tabletop in your work area should be waist high. This height is best for preventing tired arms and shoulders, and also provides the best control for straightening paper clips.

A piece of felt and a box to hold tools are key for your worktable. While making jewelry place beads onto the felt to keep them from rolling onto the floor and to make pick-up easier when you are finished.

Paper Clips

Lucky you! There are tons of different kinds of paper clips on the market today. The aisles of craft and hobby stores, office supply stores, and the back-to-school section of large stores are filled with a variety of paper clips: gold; silver; copper; bright or pastel plastics; striped; or even round, square, and oversized clips.

Be aware that some clips are easier to bend than others, and that some require beads with bigger holes than others. Plastic-covered clips or oversized clips require beads with very big holes, so plan accordingly! Make sure that you decide beforehand what you would like to make with each clip, so that you have the right size bead on hand.

Practice bending clips you want to use before beginning your projects. Some clips are too difficult to straighten and will need to be used as is, some break when you try to bend them, while others bend easily into just about any shape and can be used for lots of different projects.

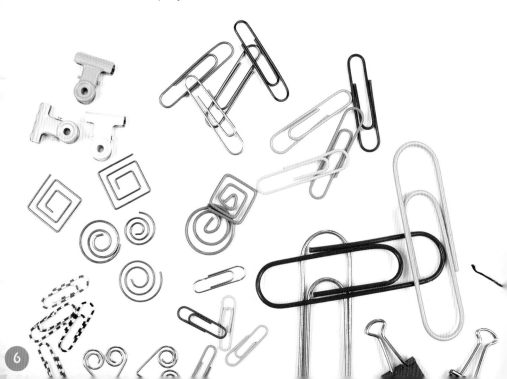

Stringing Stuff

Projects can be made with elastic, cord (leather or rattail), ribbon, string, or fine wire. Make sure the item used to string your beads is strong enough to hold them, fits through the bead holes, and does not kink.

We recommend that you have a selection of elastics, ribbons, and fine wires on hand during your jewelry making. These items can be purchased at your local craft and hobby store, are inexpensive, and will be used often.

Designer Tip: When stringing beads onto something other than a paper clip, make sure you cut your wire or string at least one-and-a-half to two times as long as the length needed. The extra length will make finishing off the ends much easier.

Beads - Charms - Embellishments

Beads, charms and embellishments come in every shape, size, and color imaginable. Some are funky, elegant, cute, bright or pastel and made from glass, plastic, crystal or metal. Some are expensive and some are not.

When selecting the beads that you are going to use, be sure that the hole is big enough to use with your paper clip, yet not so big that it can't be worn for a bracelet or necklace.

Crimp Beads

Crimp beads are small metal beads used in jewelry making that are "crimped" with pliers to keep beads in place. They are available in silver-plated, sterling sliver, gold, or copper, and come in a variety of sizes to fit any stringing material.

Clasps

A clasp is anything that holds the jewelry ends together. This can be as simple as tying a knot in the elastic or ribbon, or as professional as a metal fastener. If you decide to tie your elastic or wire ends to the clasp, place a tiny spot of glue onto the knot to secure.

Miscellaneous Stuff

Jewelry glue to hold elastic knots and/or fabric glue to hold string knots; clear fingernail polish for string ends; masking tape; glasses for safety reasons; scissors; black fine tip marker; plain paper; pencil; ruler; a piece of felt; and objects for bending clips around, such as varying widths of markers, chop sticks, or a knitting needle.

designer technique

Attaching Clasps:

The easiest way to keep a clasp permanent is to follow these easy steps:

1. Cut stringing material.

2. String 4 to 6 beads, a crimp bead, and one section of clasp.

3. Take end of stringing material and feedback through crimp bead and four to six beads.

4. Press crimp bead with pliers.

5. Continue to bead.

6. Once finished stringing beads, add a second crimp bead and the other end of clasp.

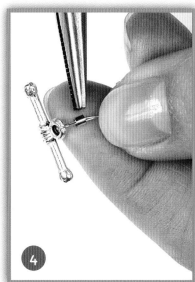

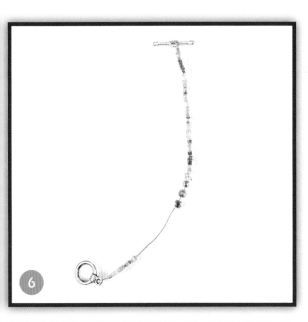

7. Feed end of stringing material back through the crimp bead and four to six beads, as done in Step 3.

8. Use pliers to pull end of string material tight so that beads meet.

9. Press second crimp bead.

10. Using scissors or wire cutters, cut end of stringing material.

Designer Tip: When stringing your beads, be sure you finish off one end before you begin stringing so that the beads do not fall off.

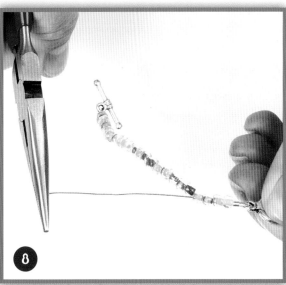

Jewelry Tools

Needle-nose pliers will help you bend, grip, and straighten paper clips and wires. If pliers are flat in your hand and you squeeze your fingers closed, the pliers will close. Once you loosen your grip, the pliers will open.

Flat-nose pliers are nice to have, but not essential. They help with crimping beads and straightening paper clips. They are also of great assistance when a second hand is needed to hold the paper clip while it is wrapped or beaded.

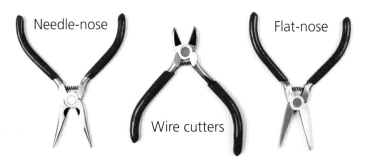

Needle-nose

Flat-nose

Wire cutters

Note: Pliers can pinch! So, be very careful when using them. If you are unsure how to use them, ask someone to show you the first time. It is so much better to be safe than sorry!

Wire Cutters: Wire cutters will cut paper clips and wires. They work exactly like your needle-nose pliers. Just place your wire against the inside of the cutters and snip.

BE CAREFUL! Sometimes, when cutting the end of a wire it can "flip" into your eye or off the table and onto the floor. We recommend that you wear a pair of glasses or safety glasses when using wire cutters. Again, it is better to be safe than sorry. If it is too difficult to cut a paper clip, have someone stronger cut it for you.

Making a Paper Clip Chain:

1. Place one or more beads on inside prong of a paper clip. Hold clip tightly in one hand or with flat-nose pliers, and use needle-nose pliers to bend tip 90 degrees. This will keep beads on the clip.

2. Bend the outside prong of clip into the clip at a 90-degree angle.

3. Add as many clips as you need to create your chain.

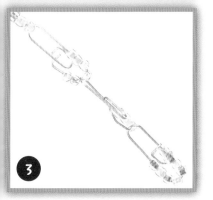

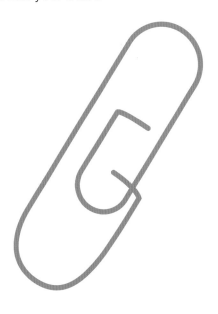

Straightening Paper Clips:

1. Use your fingers to open a paper clip into a wide V- or S-shape (see diagram below).

2. Place needle-nose or flat-nose pliers in the first bend and straighten.

3. Place needle-nose pliers into second bend and straighten.

4. To completely straighten clip, place needle-nose or flat-nose pliers on clip and rest pliers on tabletop. Squeeze pliers tightly, then release. Move pliers a tiny bit, squeeze again, and repeat to end of clip.

Note: It is almost impossible to create a perfectly flat clip, but if there are any noticeable bends, squeeze tightly with pliers on bend to straighten.

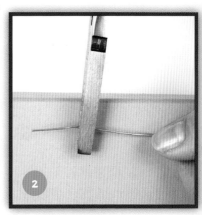

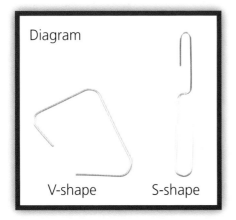

Diagram

V-shape   S-shape

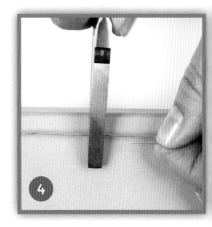

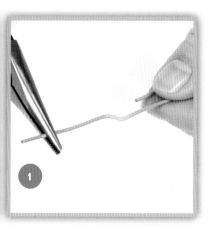

Bending Paper Clips:

1. Straighten paper clip using needle-nose or flat-nose pliers (see page 14).

2. Bend end of clip 90° with needle-nose pliers.

3. Put needle-nose pliers just to right of angle, and bend clip to close loop.

   Note: If you are going to use the loop to attach to something, do not angle second bend completely closed until loop is attached. Continue to close bend.

   Designer Tip: If you need to open a loop, bend second angle straight out—do not pull it sideways or twist. Do not open loop any wider than necessary to attach it to object. You may want to practice this so that you do not break the bend once you have added all of your beads.

RINGS

1. To make a basic ring or circle, first straighten paper clip (see page 14). Use your fingers to bend clip around an object that is the size of the circle needed. If making a ring, you will want the object to be the size of your finger.

Note: The object you are using to bend the paper clip around could be a marker, a chopstick or knitting needle, or special jewelry tools that can be purchased for this process.

2. Twist ends of paper clip over object. Now slide circle off of object.

3. If using the circle for something wearable, like a ring, slip a bead on each end of paper clip.

4. Clip excess and then bend tips under the beads. This will keep ends from being sharp and uncomfortable.

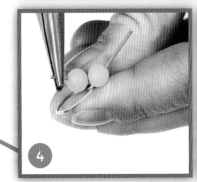

SQUARES - CIRCLES - TRIANGLES

1. Straighten paper clip and make End Loop (see pages 14-15). Starting about ¼″ (.25cm) from End Loop, make a bend using needle-nose pliers. Continue making bends, farther and farther apart. At the end, make a second End Loop that is NOT completely closed.

Note: Squares & circles can be perfectly square and round or more free form.

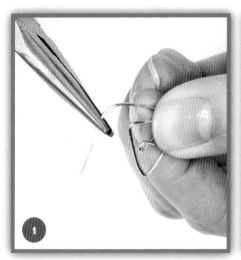

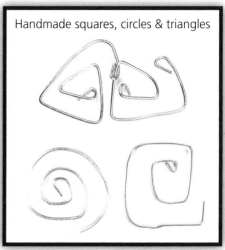

Handmade squares, circles & triangles

2. Paper clip circles can be made the same way.

Designer Secret: To add a clasp to your shaped paper clip piece, slightly open first End Loop, slip on clasp end of closure, and close End Loop. At opposite end of paper clip chain, slightly open End Loop and slip ring into End Loop, then close.

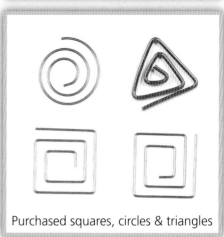

Purchased squares, circles & triangles

TRIANGLES

1. Straighten paper clip and make End Loop (see pages 14-15).

2. Create a triangle template (like the one shown) that is the desired size of your finished triangle.

3. Place straightened clip along template. Use black marker to place a dot on clip at first corner of triangle template.

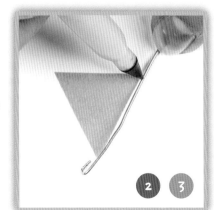

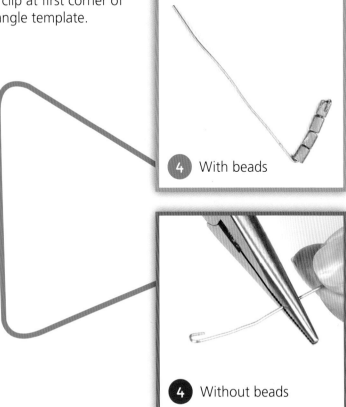

4. With beads

4. Without beads

4. (String beads, if desired.) Bend first corner of triangle at dot.

5. Repeat Steps 3–4 for second corner, (adding beads if wanted) bending into triangle shape.

6. (Add beads on final arm of triangle if wanted.) Make second End Loop that is NOT completely closed. Slip into first End Loop, close.

With beads

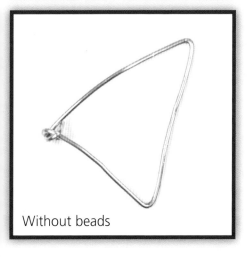

Without beads

ZIGZAGS

1. Straighten paper clip and make End Loop (see pages 14-15).

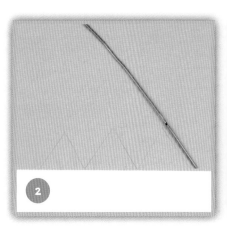

2. Make a template of zigzags the size you want them to be.

   Note: If zigzags are used for a necklace, they may be larger and spaced farther apart than if using them for a bracelet.

   Lay clip on template, mark first bend with black marker, and make a bend using needle-nose pliers.

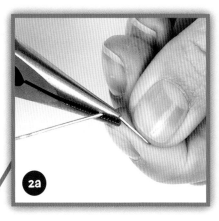

3. Repeat until all bends are made. Finish with second End Loop.

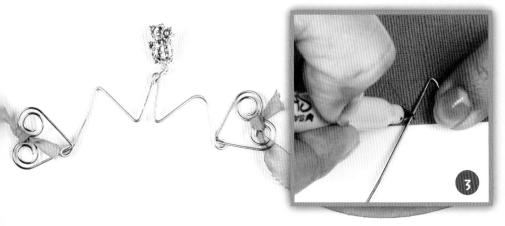

TWISTS

1. Straighten paper clip and make End Loop (see pages 14-15).

2. Use needle-nose pliers to turn clip in any direction and wrap parts of clip around a nail, knitting needle, or chop stick.

Note: It is easier to vary twists, instead of trying to make them uniform.

3. Make End Loop on other end.

Designer Tip: You can create tons of these little twists, then link them together to form bracelets, necklaces, or bag handles.

LOOP-DE-LOOPS

1. Straighten paper clip and make End Loops on both ends (see pages 14-15). Lay a thick marker, knitting needle, or other object of desired size on top of the clip.

Note: If adding small beads to loop-de-loop, string beads onto straightened paper clip before setting marker or knitting needle onto clip.

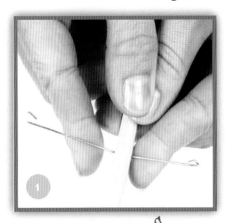
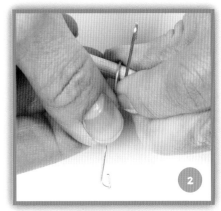

2. Use your thumbs to wrap the prongs of the paper clip tightly over top of object until a complete circle is formed.

3. Slide off.

Designer Secret: Try adding beads; paper clip triangles, circles, and squares; or charms.

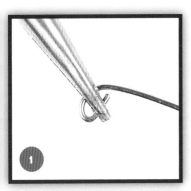

SPIRALS

1. Straighten paper clip (see page 14). Bend a tiny loop like End Loop on page 15, but smaller. Take tiny loop and clamp between pliers, so that paper clip points to the side.

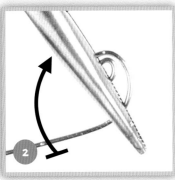

2. Tightly squeeze pliers and push paper clip up towards pliers with your finger.

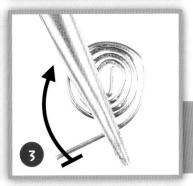

3. Move clip in pliers, and repeat Step 2 until spiral is complete.

   Note: This takes a little practice to get spirals to be somewhat even, so we recommend practicing on a few clips.

Designer Tip: If you are going to connect spirals to something, you will need to make an End Loop at one end of each spiral or you can wrap circles together with thin wire.

Designer Secret: If you are going to add beads to spiral, make spiral looser and add beads after spiral is made.

COILS

1. Straighten paper clip and make one End Loop (see pages 14-15). Lay knitting needle, chop stick, or object of similar size across paperclip to form an X.

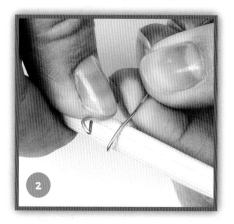 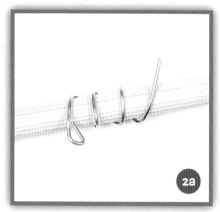

2. Use your thumbs to wrap prongs of clip around needle, keeping wraps close together.

3. Pull needle through wraps. Use needle-nose pliers to bend end of clip in line with the rest of the coils.

Designer Secret: If you want to add beads to coils, string beads onto wire before you wrap coils. Otherwise, you will only be able to add beads to the end of the coils.

Designer Tip: You can straighten your coils so that your spiral clips lie evenly, or you can stretch it so that the coils take a different shape.

WRAPS

1. Straighten paper clip (see page 14). Put paper clip through bead and twist into a form of double End Loop.

2. Hold the edge of a bead near end of paper clip. Begin to crisscross or wrap paper clip around bead.

3. Take end of paper clip and bend into double End Loop, wrap paper clip end around Loop or push into bead.

Note: There is no right or wrong way to wrap your bead.

Designer Secret: Try twisting wires as you wrap around bead.

Finished wrapped bead

Chapter 2
Paper Clip Treasures

Paper Clip Flowers

1. Use the smallest paper clips that you can find. Straighten one paper clip for the flower's center, and one for each petal (see page 14). Draw a diagram of the flower shape you want your jewelry piece to be (flower shapes can vary as desired).

2. Gently bend other paper clips the shape and size of the diagram. Place the paper clip petals on diagram to see if ends need to be trimmed. Make certain you leave enough on each end to make an End Loop, which will connect petals to paper clip circle. Make all of your petals, connect them to circle, and clip any excess at ends.

3. Bend one paper clip into a circle. Bend partially closed End Loops (see page 15) on each petal, then place End Loops over flower center wire circle and close End Loops.

4. To make center of flower, cut a piece of heavy cardstock, matte board, or use tiny circle of tin purchased from a local craft and hobby store. Adhere this circle to the top of paper clip circle with metal adhesive. Cover center with beads, rhinestones, pom-poms, or whatever your imagination desires.

Designer Tip: These can be used for pieces of jewelry, pins, magnets, or barrettes.

Designer Secret: Pape
clips can be bent into any
shape. Draw your shape
the size you want it.
Open paper clips and
bend around shape,
adding beads as you go.

Bookmarks

We read, we do homework, we flip through magazines, then we lose our place. These paper clip bookmarks will help you pick up right where you left off, so you never have to read that last chapter twice!

Designer Tip: Metal bookmarks may be purchased at craft stores.

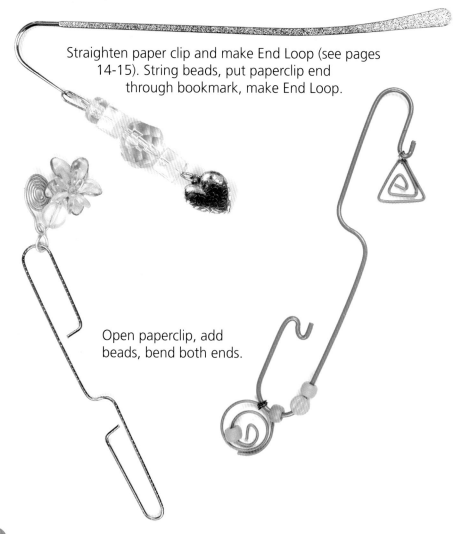

Straighten paper clip and make End Loop (see pages 14-15). String beads, put paperclip end through bookmark, make End Loop.

Open paperclip, add beads, bend both ends.

bye-bye
healthy
ionships.

A loyal

There are people who
take the heart out of you,
and there are people who
put it back.

Key Rings

Most of us spend too much time looking for our keys. How do they manage to lose themselves on a daily basis? With these fancy key rings, you can hang them on a hook where you know right where to look, or they will simply be easier to spot lying among your homework.

Partially open clip and add bead or charm.

Straighten paper clip, make one End Loop and wrap around key ring. Close End Loop (see pages 14-15). String beads, partially bend End Loop, add charm, continue to bend End Loop around key ring.

Grocery List

Bottle & Glass Charms

It's your party and everyone keeps leaving their bottle or glasses of soda everywhere. And, of course, no one can remember which one is his or hers. With these new little bottle and glass charms, each of your guests will know exactly which is theirs. They will have fun choosing the charm they like the most.

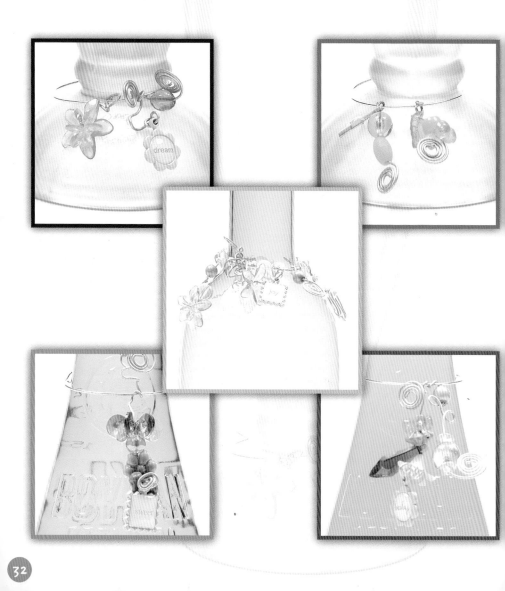

Straighten paper clip and make End Loop (see pages 14-15). Bend paper clip into a circle that will fit around the bottle or glass stem. Add beads and bent paper clip shapes. Make an End Loop but do not close completely so guests can hook rings around their glass or bottle.

Sun Catchers

Sun catchers make everyone smile. These prisms dance on the wall and add sparkle to even the most ordinary of days.

Make a paper clip chain (see page 13), make End Loop (see page 15), add beads or charms, make End Loop, attach.

Make a paper clip chain of circles (see pages 13 & 17).

Straighten paper clips and bend into a star shape (see pages 26-27). Attach to chain with End Loop (see pages 14-15).

Designer Tip: When beading a long strand of paper clips, tape one end to the table to prevent tangling.

Lamp Pulls and Fringe

Decorating your room can be expensive and time consuming—want an easy yet fancy change? Add beaded fringe to your lamp shade and decorative pulls to lamps and fans. They are what you will notice first, so all of a sudden your room will look like a designer has been there while you were in class.

Make a paper clip chain (see page 13), add beads or charms at end of chain. Cut off ¼ (.635cm) of a straightened paper clip and make EndLoopthroughcharm,addbead, close End Loop, attach to lamp.

Open paper clip into a S-shape (see page 14), add beads, bend one end at 90° angle, bend second end 90°, poke through lamp shade, carefully bend end down to secure in shade.

Bag Tags

Putting your name on your purse, backpack, or carry-on bag is a really good idea. These "luggage tags" will give the information needed if you forget and leave your bag somewhere or will simply add a designer touch!

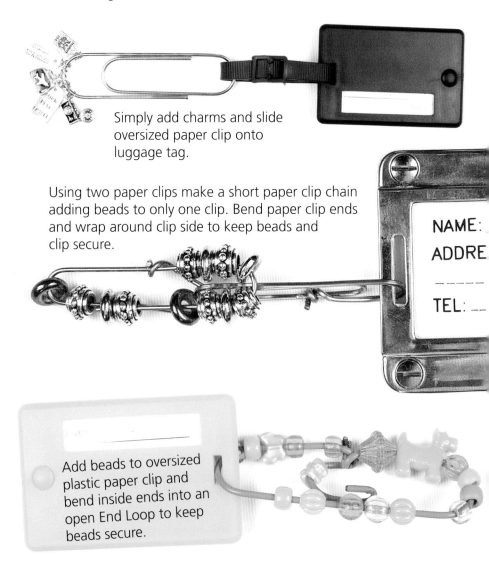

Simply add charms and slide oversized paper clip onto luggage tag.

Using two paper clips make a short paper clip chain adding beads to only one clip. Bend paper clip ends and wrap around clip side to keep beads and clip secure.

NAME:
ADDRE
TEL: __

Add beads to oversized plastic paper clip and bend inside ends into an open End Loop to keep beads secure.

Straighten paper clip, add beads, make End Loop after sliding paper clip through tag and wrap end, make circle on other end (see pages 14,15 & 17).

Straighten paper clip and make End Loop (see pages 14-15). Coil paper clip (see page 24), add charm and name tag, attach to luggage or handbag.

Paper Clip Shapes

Paper clip shapes can be used for jewelry, to adorn greeting cards, or for whatever you can imagine. Draw shapes, write words, and bend straightened clips around your patterns. Add beads as you go (see pages 14, 26-27).

This **butterfly body** is made by straightening a paper clip & making an End Loop, (see pages 14-15). String beads onto straightened clip & make End Loop.

Draw **butterfly wings**, straighten additional paper clips, bend around drawing, beading as you bend.

For **antenna**, straighten paper clip, make End Loop, bead, make End Loop, attach.

Wings can be left open or can be filled in by attaching thin wire to wing sides and loop, bead, twist wire through wing shape.

x

39

Gift Tags

Making cute tags is fun, but don't stop there. Attach them to a bag or present using beaded paper clips. You can even make your bag paper clip fancy by straightening your paper clips, adding beads, and twisting in and out of the bag sides. You can even make a fancy handle to match.

Back to School

Nothing makes you happier than pretty things… and your notebooks are no exception. They come in such wonderful colors and patterns, why not add one more personal touch and decorate them with beaded paper clips?

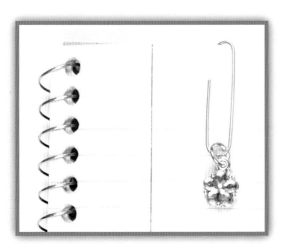

It is so easy to make something "fancy." Simply add charms, beads, or buttons to paper clips.

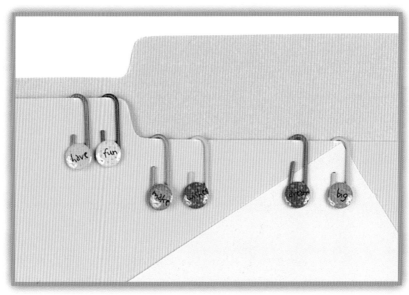

Zipper pulls
are that extraordinary touch
to plain school or make-up bags. Bead clips, bend in
shapes, add charms, it is all such fun!

Add charms, beads, or buttons to plain paper clips, office clips, or markers for a little something special.

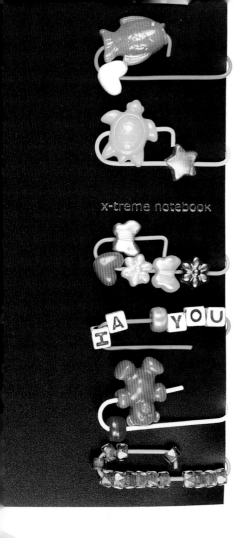

x-treme notebook

These are fun to make and keep or to give your friends or teachers to brighten their day.

Chapter 3
Paper Clip Jewelry

Pins!

These cute little pins are very fun to make. Adding a charm to a paper clip that reminds you of a particular friend can make friendship pins. Have each friend make her own paper clip for you, slide paper clips on an oversized pin, tie on a bow with pin back glued on, and this will soon become one of you most treasured pieces of jewelry.

Make a cute dress pin. Cut front and back pattern out of cardstock adding front and back tabs at the shoulder to fold and glue together. Straighten a paper clip and bend it into a hanger (see pages 14, 26-27). Glue shoulder tabs together, insert hanger, attach a pin back, now make one for all your friends.

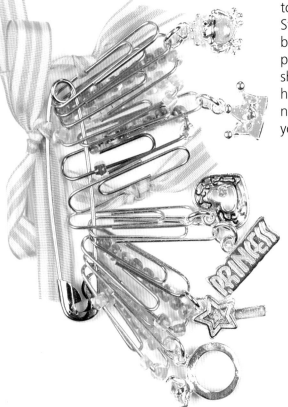

When you think of pins, you probably think of your grandmother. Fashionable pins tend to come and go, but pins are so "IN" right now. Make one to set off a plain jacket or coat. You will be the girl who everyone else tries to dress like!

Make a pin for Mom just to say "I Love You." Straighten paper clips (see page 14), cover with beads, bend in a petal shape leaving a stem on each petal (see pages 26-27). Bring all petal stems together in center and wrap with florist tape or ribbon. Tie flowers with a bow, add pin back, and give it to your Mom - on just an ordinary Tuesday!

Make a "charm pin." Slide charms onto a larger paper clip, tie a bow, and add a pin back to the back of bow. Making a statement has never been so easy, or so pretty!

Necklaces and Bracelets

Necklaces seem to be the most admired of all jewelry but every necklace needs a matching bracelet. Everyone notices a beautiful or extraordinary necklace. Make just one or make a bunch and wear them all together… all of the models and stars are doing it!

Make a lady bug from cardstock, straighten a paper clip (see page 14) and make the antenna, glue to lady bug and glue lady bug to a chain. You can also make bees, butterflies, or flowers.

Connect large metal rings with paper clip circles (see page 17). Tie a ribbon on both ends and you have a designer necklace.

Straighten several paper clips and make End Loops (see pages 14-15), connect these together into a bracelet. Straighten additional paper clips; add beads; bend into spirals, circles, zigzags, and squares (see pages 16-19, 23-24); wrap around bracelet.

A triangle necklace and bracelet are easy and fun to make (see page 19 for "how to").

Paper clip jewelry can be as plain or as fancy as you want. Straighten paper clips (see page 14) and bend into shapes (see pages 26-27), add pieces of a chain and beads, make End Loops (see page 15). The result is totally stunning!

Paper clip flowers make very cute ribbon bracelets and chokers (see pages 26-27).

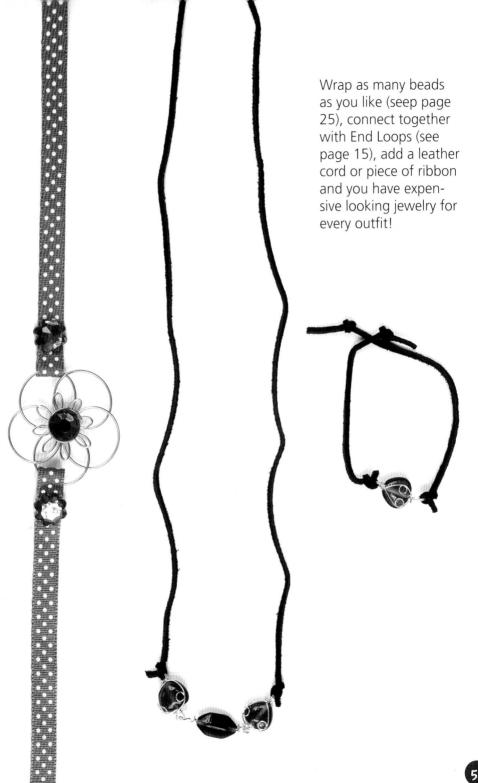

Wrap as many beads as you like (seep page 25), connect together with End Loops (see page 15), add a leather cord or piece of ribbon and you have expensive looking jewelry for every outfit!

Bracelets

Bracelets can be a subtle embellishment, or make quite the statement. Mix it up—wear them one at a time, or all together.

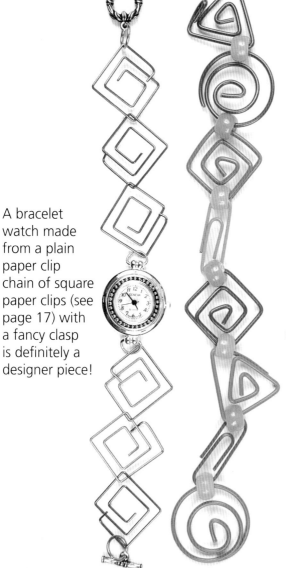

A bracelet watch made from a plain paper clip chain of square paper clips (see page 17) with a fancy clasp is definitely a designer piece!

A paper clip chain of squares, triangles, and circles is so easy you can make one for everyone you know. Straighten paper clips (see page 14); make squares, circles, and triangles (see page 17), connect shapes by sliding end of shape or plain paper clip through a bead; add End Loop (see page 15) on one end of chain.

Make two beaded triangles (See pages 18-19). Tie together in the center by putting a thin wire through a larger bead and wrap triangles together. Add beaded wire straps (see pages 10-11) and you have a lovely piece of jewelry for the school dance!

A paper clip chain of circle shapes can be made into a bracelet, an anklet, a necklace, or a belt. Straighten paper clips (see page 14) and make into circles (see page 17), wire circles together by wrapping two circles together with tiny pieces of wire, add crimp beads at the end of each paper clip to hold beads on the paper clip, and wire clasp on with tiny pieces of wire.

Open up your ▶ plastic covered paper clips into a S-shape, add Fimo clay beads, connect with End Loops (see page 15) and you have a piece of jewelry that is fun for the beach or after-school party!

Earrings

Earrings make the outfit, so
you must have a pair to match
each one. After all, your face
is the first thing that someone
sees when they look at you, and
your earrings will frame your
face. Make that first impression
memorable, beautiful,
and fashionable.

◄ Single beaded
triangle ear-
rings (see
pages 18-19).

▲ Wrapped
crystal earrings
(see page 25).

Wire rings in a paper clip
circle (see page 17).

"Charm" earrings are as much fun to make and wear as charm bracelets. Follow instructions for Charm Pin on page 46 but slip clips onto a large ring that is connected to an earring holder. Your new earrings are personable, fashionable, and irresistible!

Simple charm earrings are easy and changeable – just slip on new charms for each new occasion. Straighten paper clips (see page 14) and make into circles (see page 17), slide charm onto paper clips, and slide paper clips onto earring holders.

Initials

Initials personalize everything. Make them and hang them from a chain for a necklace, on your door, or in your window.

Straighten your paper clip (see page 14), draw your initials, bend paper clip to match drawing (see page 26-27). To connect two points make an End Loop on connecting piece (see page 15). Thread pearls or beads onto thin wire and wrap around your paper clip initial.

Rings, Rings, Rings, For Fingers and Toes

Finger and foot fashion are a must. They simply make you feel completely put together. And these are so simple to make that you can have one to match every outfit. You will be the envy of all of your friends.

Straighten paper clip and make a ring (see pages 14, 16); add beads, charms, or bent paper clip shapes (see page 49), and *voilà*...you can have a ring for every-day of the week!

Belts

Belts can definitely make a fashion statement. The fancier they are, the more they are "oohed" and "ahhed" over. Be somebody special. Make a statement. Wear a really great belt!

Make a belt by creating a paper clip chain and tying paper clips together with a piece of ribbon. Create a "belt latch" by opening two paper clips into an "S" and making one End Loop (see pages 14-15).

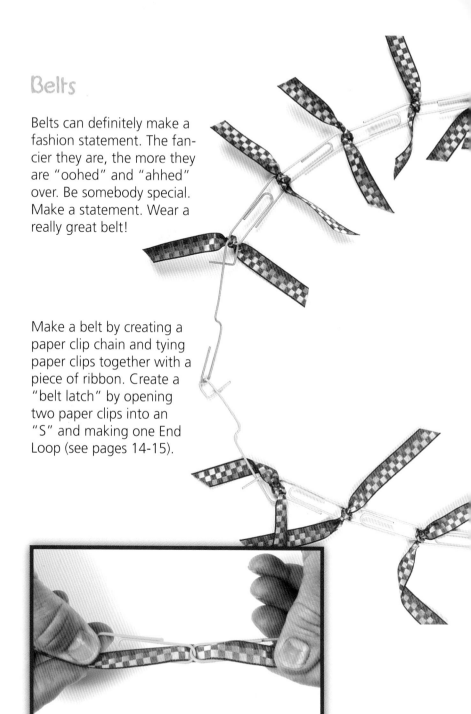

Zipper Pulls

Zippers are zippers—plain but necessary, and they are sometimes hard to pull. Add a paper clip pull to a bag or to the front of a jacket or coat—it will go instantly from ordinary to designer, from inexpensive to wearable art!

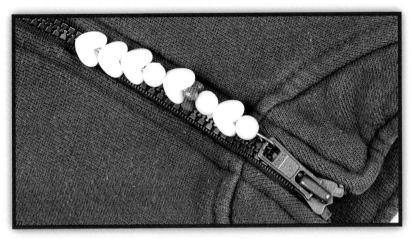

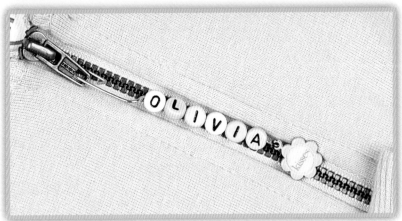

To make zipper pulls straighten paper clip, add beads, and make End Loop (see pages 14-15). One End Loop hooks through the zipper.

Once you wear a zipper pull your outfits will be just too plain without them!

To make these three zipper pulls straighten paper clip and make End Loop (see pages 14-15). String beads, add a shaped paper clip, a charm, or the shells are an earring without out a mate.

Straighten paper clip and make End Loops (see pages 14-15). Twist clip in a coil (see page 24), and add a charm.

Straighten a paper clip and make End Loops (see pages 14-15, make a zig zag (see page 20), hook onto paper clip with a glass bead.

Straighten paper clip and make End Loops (see pages 14-15). Make a paper clip chain (see page 13). On one end of chain attach two crystals and on other end of chain attach a "S" shaped paper clip with End Loop to hang in zipper.

Jean Jewelry

Straighten paper clips (see page 14) and make into circles (see page 17), add charms to circles. Straighten another paper clip, add beads and End Loops (see page 15). Hook all pieces to belt buckle.

For Pocket Chain make same paper clip circles and same beaded paper clips. Hook into chain with small pieces of wire. Hang from paper clip clipped onto jean pocket.

Jean Jewelry is easy, fun, and looks so expensive. Add charms to your paper clips and your jewelry and your jeans will let everyone know who you are and what you like.

Add charms and beads attached to small pieces of chain to colored paper clips, slip clips onto key hook, hang hook from belt, loop and tie piece of ribbon over loop.

Practice

Ever heard the saying "Practice makes perfect?" Well, we recommend that if you have never made jewelry, or are unfamiliar with a certain technique, that you practice on a discardable paper clip or bead before using the one meant to be part of your jewelry. This simple precaution could save you a second trip to the store to buy another must-have material.

Designer Tip: When bending and straightening paper clips your hands can become tired. If they do begin to feel tired or cramped, give them a break. To loosen them up, stretch your hands, squeeze your fists closed, then open wide. Repeat a few times and as often as needed.